KING MIDAS

Illustrated by Kristen Goeters
Adapted by Jennifer Boudart

Louis Weber, C.E.O.
Publications International, Ltd.
7373 North Cicero Avenue
Lincolnwood, Illinois 60646

Manufactured in U.S.A.

ISBN: 0-7853-1924-7

PUBLICATIONS INTERNATIONAL, LTD.
Stories to Grow On is a trademark of Publications International, Ltd.

There once was a king named Midas, who ruled a magical land of roses and sunshine. Midas was rich beyond imagination, but he was also selfish and foolish. Instead of enjoying the warm sunshine and wonderful flowers in his beautiful kingdom, King Midas spent his days locked in a room all by himself, counting his money.

There was nothing that Midas would rather do than count his riches. Every day he got up at the crack of dawn and headed straight to his gold. And every night he would lie awake dreaming of how to get more.

King Midas had a beautiful daughter named
Marygold. She was very different from her father.
Marygold did not care much for gold, and she
was not at all selfish. Day after day Marygold
walked happily among the roses in the garden.
It was her favorite place. She loved taking care of
all the beautiful flowers and watering them so
they would grow to be even taller than she was.
There was nothing Marygold liked better than
smelling the sweet scent of the roses and watching
the pretty butterflies in her garden.

Marygold was sorry that her father never
joined her. She wished he would leave his gold
and come outside to enjoy the garden.

One day Midas was counting his gold when a stranger appeared. "How did you get in here?" asked King Midas.

"Well," said the stranger, "I have some magical powers. My, you certainly have a lot of gold."

"I could always use more," said Midas.

"I could give you the power to turn all that you touch into gold," said the stranger.

Midas excitedly said, "Yes, yes! I would like that very much."

The stranger told Midas that after the next sunrise, anything he touched would turn to gold.

King Midas spent that night sitting by the window, waiting for the sun to rise. When the dawn's light finally appeared, he reached to push away the curtain. The curtain turned to solid gold! Then Midas grabbed his chair, and it was gold, too! The king ran from room to room, and everything he touched turned to gold—tables, mirrors, candlesticks, paintings, and doors.

Then Midas rushed from his castle into Marygold's garden. He knew that this was his daughter's favorite place. Midas laid his hands on a rose, and it turned from scarlet red to gold. How delighted Marygold will be, he thought, and then he turned all the roses to gold.

Soon the king's stomach began to rumble. Making gold had made him hungry! Midas returned to his castle and ordered a splendid breakfast. Servants brought plates piled high with fruit, bread, meats, and eggs. King Midas decided to start with a strawberry, but as soon as he touched it, the strawberry changed to gold and could not be eaten. Then he grabbed a goblet of water and raised it to his lips, but the water turned to gold, too! Midas became dizzy with hunger. He wanted food, but it all turned to gold! Suddenly Marygold came into the room. She held a single gold rose and was crying.

Marygold sat at the table with her father and sobbed. "Look at this poor rose," she said. "How could this have happened?"

"I made it happen," answered King Midas. "Don't you like it?"

"My roses are ruined!" exclaimed Marygold. "They do not smell sweet. They do not feel like velvet. They do not make butterflies dance. They are worthless!"

Like all fathers, King Midas was very sad that his daughter was unhappy, and he wanted to make her feel better. Without thinking he rushed over to her and gave her a comforting hug. As soon as he did, Marygold turned to gold!

King Midas ran from his golden daughter. He now knew his wish had been a curse, not a blessing. If only he could turn back time, then he could get his beautiful daughter back.

Just then the stranger returned and asked, "Aren't you pleased with all your gold?"

"I was very foolish," said King Midas. "Save my daughter, and you can have all my gold."

"I do not want your gold, Midas. I just wanted to teach you a lesson. To get your daughter back, go to the river just beyond the rose garden. Dive into its waters and bring back enough water to sprinkle over all the things you have turned to gold. They will return to normal."

King Midas called all his servants, "Gather every pail and bucket you can find, and bring them to the river!" Without another word he ran to the river's edge and leaped into the cold, rushing water.

The water around the king began to turn golden yellow. He watched as the golden layer fell to the bottom of the river. Quickly King Midas filled several pails with water and returned to the castle. He went straight to the dining hall and splashed water over every golden object, including his daughter. When King Midas saw Marygold change back to her normal self, his heart filled with joy.

King Midas was very thankful to have his daughter back. Together they went outside and changed all the gold flowers back to beautiful red roses. Midas had learned that there are much more important things in life than gold.

From that day on, King Midas was happier than he had ever been before. He no longer spent his days locked away all by himself. Instead he liked to go outdoors, where he could water the flowers and watch the butterflies dance with his most valuable treasure, Marygold.

The only gold that King Midas cared for now was the gold of the sunshine.

One to Grow On

Wisdom

Wisdom is learning to make the right choices. This story shows us that it is not always easy to do the wise thing. King Midas loved gold and thought the more he had, the happier he would be. A wise person knows that money or gold can't buy happiness and that simple things can be best. In the end King Midas grew wiser. He found out that gold did not make him happy and that the best things in life—his daughter, flowers, and the warm sunshine—are free.